Fluffy Socks

Poems
by
Drew Lankford

for my great teachers
seeing in me something
I didn't know was there

Dear Reader

Thanks for being with me. It's good to have someone to travel with. Life is hard sometimes, nearly unbearable, but the sunlight always appears, clears the sky, warms and brightens the world. Getting through the bad and into the good is what it's all about after all. Take my hand; it's a calm night and only a short walk. Who knows what we may discover on the way.

D W B   P U B L I S H I N G
www.dancingwithbearpublishing.com

fear

I'm afraid;
there you go,
hurl a brick at my face
if you like,
I admit it.
Knowing God doesn't give a spirit
of fear certainly isn't helping
rid me of this fear right now.
Knowing and *knowing*
are two different creatures.
Could be I've strayed
so far from the good path
I can never return;
no clue.
The more I think about it
the more my head hurts.
One thing's for sure,
I'm afraid,
makes me feel better saying it,
opening my chest
to the torches
and eyes of the world.
If I don't live to see another day,
at least I had the guts
to come out and say
I was afraid,
and in my book
that's saying something.

crab legs

Seated around a table
inside a Chinese restaurant
a family cracks open crab legs,
pulls shreds of meat with tiny forks.
Nearly exhausted from a long day,
the mother pulls out
a super long piece of meat;
she feels like she's hit the lottery.
As if watching a body
scramble from a grave,
everyone- even the dishwasher
sneaking a smoke
in the corner-
falls into silence.
She pours hot butter over the meat,
slides it into her mouth.

On this rainy Wednesday night,
when things like this
aren't supposed to happen,
the family continues opening crab legs
under strings of festive lights,
pretending to enjoy,
but their hearts
spin through their bodies
like tornadoes through fields of wheat.

getting lost

He's walked this path
in the woods so often
he can do it with his eyes shut.
He wonders as he walks,
failures, accomplishments,
girls he wished he'd asked on dates
but chickened out.
He turns and walks back
the same way he came.
Not a sin
or sure ticket to Hell,
but an awful waste of time all the
same.
As long as fear
squeezes tightly
he'll never let go;
but the day comes
when he's had enough;
and he continues walking,
getting lost
in spite of everything he's learned.
Those girls he'd never
had the nerve to ask out
are waiting all around
with open arms,
now asking him for a date;
finding the way back home
now the farthest thing from his mind.

flaws

Flaws follow
and do us damage;
trying to avoid them,
impossible,
doesn't work that way.
Must admit them,
deal with them,
hit them head on.
Here's a bit of advice:
Scoot close enough
to tell them a joke or a line from a
poem;
that makes them furious,
but brings brief rest;
when they surround
and jump on you,
slashing anything
they can sink their blades into,
pretend to know what's up;
for some reason
it makes them cringe and release
when they think we know more than
they do.
Hate that for them; don't you?
Don't get cocky;
they'll soon be back;
the next move is on you my friend.

fighting it

A horse walks down a road.
The rider of the horse pulls
back his hood, inhales cold

air, holds it in his lungs. He
stops at a small house, thinking
how painful it will be to go

to the grocery store later. He
exhales the cold air from his
lungs. It moves like sad mist,

searching and finding cracks
in the walls of the house, entering
the mouth of a sleeping child.

The child stops breathing;
not long after, screams erupt
from the young mother inside.

The rider pats his horse;
the horse seems to understand.
They cross the valley near his

home. Hearing the screams,
and putting hands to his ears,
he prays the price of groceries

have dropped so he'll have at
least a few dollars left after
cashing his measly paycheck.

16

The screams get louder;
he keeps his hands on his ears,
grows angrier at his wife for not

going to the store earlier like
she'd promised, choosing instead
to have her hair curled and nails

painted. His hands shake; the
screams persist, always do;
but he's fighting it.

If worth anything, at this
time of night the lines at the
grocery store are usually short.

wait and see

I'm a good girl,
done nothing wrong.
I climb the hill,
shout as loudly as I can,
longing for this pain to ease.
Walking down the hill
I realize I'm alone,
will never get much help
on this path I've not chosen.
I'm a good girl,
done nothing wrong,
worthy of a good life,
a nice man,
children,
a pretty house.
I hate hiding like a scared rabbit.
They say think on better things,
things that will make
my mind and heart more pure,
but they don't understand
the difference between
what should and can be done.
Some things are out of my control.
I'm a good girl,
done nothing wrong.
I'll get my moment in the sun;
just you wait and see.

human thing

We go back
expecting new results,
but it's always the same thing,
pleasure for a moment,
pain for the day.
Disappointing,
the same salty wind
stinging and cutting our faces
until skull remains.
Maybe this once,
instead of going
back expecting new results,
we trudge ahead.
Surely the sky
wouldn't collapse if we did.
But since going back is a flaw
we need like blood,
our human thing,
our cosmic touch,
maybe it's best
we know we have
loads more work to do
before considering such a move.

for my kids

bad thoughts
yank joy right out of us.
regardless of the pleasure
they get for doing this,
these are the cards
we're dealt and must play.
no one said
it was easy.
if you get close
to giving up,
scooting away
from the table
and cashing in,
there's hope
and love and life
and many good things
waiting just over the hillside.

another excuse

My dear,
a quick buzz to let you know
I may be late for dinner.
You see,
I'm falling down a hole,
accelerating so quickly
my clothes are burning;
don't worry,
I'm not wearing my good suit,
and the pain's not as bad
as you may think;
at least not yet;
down and down I go
like Alice down her rabbit hole.
If I was in charge of this place
I'd turn down the heat.
Surely,
just a flick of a switch
would cool things a bit.
If I can find a supervisor
after this crazy ride's over
I'm going to complain.
What harm can it do?
My dear,
I may be late for dinner,
and my face may be melted,
but don't worry,
I'll pick up the milk and eggs
for Sunday morning breakfast.
It's been a really trying day.

need

I trip
across
dark
fields,
cold,
hungry,
trembling,
begging
you to care;

I need
you to
stop,
look
me dead
in the
eyes,
see me,
not who
you want
me to be.

the right choice

Standing on the ledge
he can choose love
or he can choose hate,
but he must make a choice,
no in-between;
Doubtless,
the tiny angel and devil
perched on either side of his shoulders
will not be satisfied;
they can't, not in their DNA.
Even with these creatures
breathing on his cheeks,
whispering sweet nothings in his ears,
not much he can do
but carry on as he's carried
on since first having to make this big
decision.
The angel may pinch his ear,
the devil may flick flames from his
tongue,
but whatever stupid stunts they pull,
he will soon prove
when you get down to it,
humanity is insanely strong.

some blues

devil by my side
me at the wheel
speeding down
the big winding hill

he got my soul
one starry night
offered the moon
and all that's bright

faster we go
can't ever slow
he's got my soul
speeding down
the big winding hill

devil by my side
me at the wheel
together we sing
and always will
speeding down
the big winding hill

cute meet

A man and woman
find each other.
Liking what they see,
they share funny stories
and dark secrets.
Things go well.
But when he steps back
and trips over a garden gnome,
falling on his face,
she looks away.
Even with divine guidance
the poor man can't catch a break.
Without missing a beat,
he stands,
dusts off his clothes,
begins where he left off.
He believes he may love her;
she knows she does.

the wise man

They say be careful what you ask for.
But as usual, I'm a pickle head, don't

listen, have to make my own mistakes.
So, for kicks, I fall to my knees and
pray

for wisdom. The next morning I've got
it in droves, as well as a long scraggly
beard,

the sort of beard the sleeper in Irving's
tale, once jostled from his long sleep,

would've wanted to fiddle with. With
this new wisdom I should feel fresh and
alive,

but it's just the opposite; I feel a
throbbing headache, a bitter taste in
my mouth, and

cramping in my stomach. To make
matters worse, a man in a brown robe
arrives at my

bedside (how or when he gets there,
haven't a clue). He bows, begs for
answers to ancient

secrets. Without knowing what I'm
saying, I explain things forbidden to

say. He stands,

bows, drops coins on my bedside table
(a pleasant surprise to say the least)

and sneaks out (sure wish I knew how
he does this). What I do know,
however,

I've got to clear out of here before
word spreads and more people show up
wanting

to hear what I have to say. I've not
even started this wise man gig and
already I

realize I'm out of my league, a high
school freshman at a college party;

the problem is I can't handle
someone else sneaking into my
bedroom. Who could? Looks like
it's back to my knees to pray,

this time for more stupidity,
which I'm sure I'll get since I've

got so much stored away. I bet
I'll be pounded hard for this

prayer too, but at least I've
thought out the request clearly,
and, fingers and toes and legs
crossed, that should push me through.

flapping

A black cat
sprints across the yard
toward dark bushes,
a bird flapping in its mouth.

we are that bird,
flapping in the mouth
of the cat
sprinting across the yard
towards dark bushes,
trying to get loose
from those jaws and sharp teeth
firmly clamped.

we may never
fly and sing through the sky
as we once did,
but us flapping
in the mouth of the cat,
that makes the difference;
there's our safe ride home.

as we are

we must face
each other before
it's too late,

face each other
as we are,

gorgeous machines,
magnificently human.

the only one

Scary noises inside
the bedroom disturb
his sleep.

He tries meditating,
but there's too much
garbage rattling around
in his head.

Still hearing
those scary noises,
he jumps out of bed,
unlocks the bedroom door,
sneaks into the living room.

The only one
who's ever been there,
he's the creator
of the scary noises,
noises that have scared him
so badly for so long.

He's learned nothing
from past mistakes,
probably never will.

my place

Drying a few pots and pans, I look out
the window and see me on a monster of
a motorcycle, revving the engine, as if
showing off at a crowded beach during
Spring Break. I find and hold one of my
daughter's stuffed animals to the
window. The me outside gets the hint
and nods, understands I've grown, that
I'm not going to jump on the
motorcycle, pop open a cold one, and
head off to Vegas for a weekend of
madness and debauchery. The
temptation is here for sure, but it's not
as strong as it once was. The me
outside removes his sunglasses, hangs
his head, weeps. Feeling reborn, he
drives away slowly, a smile on his face.
Maybe this is the last time I'll see him.
Maybe this is the first of many more
visits. Who knows? Either way, I've
done the right thing and that counts for
something. I'm happy as ever, putting
the last pan away for the night, my kids
in the living room playing video games,
the smell of brownies in the oven
nearly driving us bonkers.

hearing

Back in the day
he went to every
concert he could.
Being one
of the unlucky ones,
over time,
the loud music
ruined his hearing.
Now,
when urges hit
and he craves a fix,
can't even eat
without dreaming about music,
he puts his hands
on the speakers
of his small radio,
plugs it into his soul,
taps his feet
until they cramp
and he can't
tap anymore.

a little help

Worry keeps her awake
all night again;
she gets out of bed,
goes into the kitchen,
makes a pot of coffee.
Looking out the window,
she sees someone looking in at her.
She steps out the door,
about to scream
at the intruder
to leave her yard;
before she does,
the person disappears.
Feeling strange,
as if a drug
had entered her blood stream,
she staggers through the yard,
noticing things she's never noticed
before.
She staggers back to the kitchen,
growing sleepier
as she watches
steam rise from the coffee...

on a less serious note

After making
a cup of tea,
she tells me
she can't drink it
because it looks
like the devil's dish water.
What a way to start the morning.
I've been around the
block a few times,
bruises to prove it,
but that's a new one.

I say nothing,
figuring silence
the best solution.

I may be gullible,
but some things are over the top;
Try as I might,
I don't believe the devil uses dishes.
Even if he stuffs lobsters
in his flaming mouth
on a special occasion,
what does he care
if he spills some
on the floors of hell?
He's got nothing to lose.

So, like the obedient
boy I've become,
I remake the tea,

whistling like an old sailor,
extra careful pressing
the tea bag in the boiling water
to get perfect taste and color.

I hand her the cup;
she looks inside,
smells, walks away.

Her not speaking
gets my goat like nothing else.
I want to ring her neck.
She sits on the sofa
under a blanket
holding the cup
of tea with both hands,
unaware I'm not
near as dumb as I look;
I've got her
exactly where I want her
(in the other room
away from me).

home

I don't belong;
I want to go home
and be with my children,
who I need,
and who need me.
What holds me here?

change

Things
she believed,
took great joy in,
was even willing
to suffer and die for,
she can't
bring herself
to believe in again.
She's happy
where she is,
where she's going.

together

If it's true
that pressures of life
help us shine,
then please,
explain why,
as I go through more pressure,
I'm not shining.
Am I rushing it?
Am I being punished?
Have I totally lost my mind?
By now, I should have a spark
or two under my fingernails,
a small flame under my tongue.
I refuse to believe I'm dead,
some sort of goofy corpse
moaning and stomping
through markets at midnight.
Now, that's silly.
I'm feeling something.
I go outside,
mow the yard
and water the plants;
the shine surfaces,
blazing from my heart,
(the last place I expect)
causing us to be together again.

broken radio

A boy holds
the radio to his ear,
but no sound comes from it.
I go over to where he is.
He takes the radio
from his ear
and hands it to me.
I put it to my ear; no sound.
I shake it gently,
turn a few buttons,
but still nothing.
Shaking my head,
I hand it back.
*Why are you listening
to this broken radio*? I ask.
Broken? he says.
It works fine, can't you hear?
I leave him alone
to do his thing,
groove to his groove;
even a boy listening
to a broken radio
deserves that much.

break

On cold rainy nights,
when we're fast asleep,
our souls escape our bodies
like curious teenagers
climbing out bedroom windows.

After the mess
they put up with,
they deserve a break,
a chance to get out and play
with buddies down the street.

Might as well go easy
when they return
the next morning for re-entry,
caked in mud,
smelling of smoke and beer.

We need them
as much as they need us,
all of us needing every break
we can get our hands on.

for my body

Like a father
holding the hand
of his two-year-old son
in the grocery store,
you work hard
preventing my soul
from galloping away
like a mad Mustang;
Please hear,
I appreciate it.
It means the world.
But maybe you
should lighten up,
not take yourself so seriously,
at least consider,
occasionally,
letting my soul free;
it needs fresh air,
a chance to stretch its legs,
catch some sunshine on his face.
Letting my soul free
may make things worse,
but at least
you can always say
you gave it a shot;
and that's huge.

lunch break in the park

A bird lands in the grass;
our eyes meet,
then a gorgeous flash.
My spirit leaves my body,
collides in the air
with the spirit of the bird.
Though much smaller,
it brawls like a street fighter
with cash on the line;
totally exhausted,
the bird flies away;
our spirits,
as if following cosmic orders,
are sucked back into our bodies.
I love that spirit;
wonder what it feels;
can't get it from my mind;
If the world's still standing,
I bet my next paycheck,
the bird will be back
in the grass tomorrow,
lifting its head
as I lift mine.

air show

Thousands of people sit on bleachers
and cheer and look up as airplanes zip
through the blue sky. A woman is
there, not looking up, but down at a
leaf turning in the wind. The leaf
reminds her of summer days when as a
girl she did beautiful hand-springs and
cart-wheels in her backyard. As planes
soar overhead, she focuses on the leaf
and wishes she could stand and do a
perfect back-flip, a flip that would
cause those in the bleachers to stand
and cheer. She watches the leaf,
strange in its design. A gust of wind
comes along and blows it off the
bleachers and closer to the backyard of
her youth, the backyard she'll be in
after she dies this evening, the
backyard she'll be in doing perfect
hand-springs and cartwheels whenever
she wants, the leaf always near,
swirling in the air she makes.

fluffy socks

She slides
across the kitchen floor
in her fluffy socks;
he watches
her from the corner
of the room in his fluffy socks;
as she hums *Tulsa Queen*,
their favorite song,
the first and last played at their
wedding,
he knows he's totally in love;
she can't see him.
Why he's still there
instead of being in a room in the sky
he doesn't know,
but he imagines the worst.
Then just like that
it's time for him to go;
as if being pulled,
he rises slowly to the ceiling.
He scrambles to stay,
but his hands pass
through everything he grabs.
Passing through the ceiling,
he cries for her to look up
and see him one final time.
But it doesn't work like that.
She hums and slides
across the kitchen floor
in her fluffy socks
as if nothing were happening.

Nearly through the roof,
he does the last
thing he can do,
jerks off his fluffy socks,
lets them go;
she picks them up,
holds them close to her chest,
never tells a soul.

valentine's day gift

Seated in the back
of the classroom,
a boy bangs his head
against the wall,
trying to get
the attention of a cute girl
across the room.
Oh, the things boys will do.
But she is too busy
popping gum and staring
at her nails to notice his attempts.
He doesn't realize
he doesn't have to
bang his head,
smack his face with a shoe,
or do any other crazy stunts
boys have done through centuries
to get a girl's attention.
All he has to do is be himself,
sit back, and if she's interested,
she'll come to him.
Watching the scene play out,
Cupid hovers outside the window,
cute as can be,
the little feathers
on back of his pink slippers fluttering.
He licks the tip of an arrow,
puts it to the string in the bow,
pulls back, fires.
The arrow sails through the room
like a heat seeking missile,
twisting and turning this way and that;

hearing a few shrieks,
he jams headphones in his ears,
cranks up the volume;
grinning from ear to ear,
he flies through pinkish clouds,
his pudgy cheeks flapping in the wind.

baby

baby,
you know
our love
was never love.
whatever it was,
we needed more.
tragic,
because I was into you
and you seemed into me.

baby,
looking back,
I'm glad
things worked
out the way they did;
it's hard
having to tell you that,
but it's best.

bonding

The father looks away from his son,
stares out the window, hears tiny
heartbeats of creatures in the dark
bushes.

The father looks back to his son as if
looking for an answer, lights his pipe,
puffs, allows smoke to rise from his
lips,

drift across the room. Without saying
a word, the father speaks for his son;
he turns and looks back out the
window,

lusting for creatures in the dark bushes;
The son has been here before, knows
what's about to happen, and he sees,

reflected in the window as always, his
father's face growing wild and lovely.

so much love

The father looks
into the blue eyes
of his baby girl.
Inside her eyes
he can see her soul
looking back at him,
turning its head curiously,
checking out new territory.
She falls asleep in his arms.
He holds her for a long time.
So much love in this home
devils flying close are horrified...

biggie

no biggie,
things are calm
as she walks
under moonlight
beside railroad tracks,
kicking up rocks,
just another night.
but when the train
passes slowly
and a man
presses his face
to the window,
his frosty blue eyes
seeming to probe her soul,
that's a biggie,
something to write home about.
he's gone.
but at least she saw him
looking like he needed her;
the biggest biggie
she's ever known.

for the moon

I feel bad about last night,
had a flat tire on the way

home. You looked great as
always, I'm sure. I promise,

unless something else crazy
happens, I'll be outside in

in my yard tonight, a bottle
of red wine and two glasses.

If you want (no pressure here)
you can pull me up to you so

I can touch your face and give
you a little smoochy- pooh.

If you're not comfortable with
that, it's cool, really. But I

have to tell you when it comes
to smooch-poohs, I'm a master.

I'd brighten you up like you've
never been brightened before.

searching

we
are
strange
creatures,
searching
for
love
when
we
know
exactly
where
it is.

a friend

if you
can't hold on
any longer,
decide to let go,
allow the breeze
to carry you farther
then you've been before,
never fear,
love is there,
a map in one hand,
a white rose in the other,
the thought of leaving
never crossing its mind.

new neighbor

One summer evening
in a chair under a pear tree,
an old man enjoys some peace,

until a boy in a home-made space
costume bursts out of some bushes,
scaring him half to death.

Hi, mister, he says.
I'm star boy,
come from the stars.

Here we go, thinks the old man,
another kid from the stars;
just what I need.

The old man tosses a few sticks at star
boy;
the boy spits and cusses and flips the
bird;

he dives back into the bushes,
leaving the old man in his chair

under a pear tree, happy to be able
to finally enjoy the evening.

coloring

The girl uses markers to color in her book. She also uses them to color her arms and face. She runs out of her room excited to show her mother how well she's staying inside the lines. The mother picks her up onto her lap, and gives her a kiss, causing colors to smear on her too. Instead of being angry, she feels reborn, as if immersed in ice cold water. She holds her daughter in her lap, watching her hold the markers tightly, trying so hard to color inside the lines. Closing her eyes, she wants to keep her forever. For a long time they sit there, the daughter, coloring, the mother, dreaming and knowing she must get up soon, clean the colors from their bodies, get back to the work she had been doing.

a boy and his toys

He steps outside
and picks up a laser gun
from the wet grass.
He puts it to his head,
closes his eyes,
pulls the trigger.
Instead of a laser firing
through his brain,
he only gets wet.
He throws the laser gun
on the roof of his house;
it slides down,
catches on other toys
already there.

leaving

On a morning walk
an old man stumbles
on a rock sticking out of the mud;
he hates seeing it so lonely,
wants to pull it up,
learn something from it,
but he can't bring himself
to take it from its home;
he wouldn't want that done to him.
love opens her eyes,
spreads her wings,
takes flight;
no one notices
but everyone feels.

a tough job

A girl stands
between two pillars,
arms outstretched,
preventing
the temple from falling.

She grimaces;
eyes and biceps bulging;
If the world was right
she'd be noticed
for all the days and nights
she saves the city.

But the world is not right,
and people pass
by with heads down.

She needs a break,
a night on the town,
sparkling wine,
a spin or two
on the dance floor,
something,
but her boss
doesn't see it that way,
never will.

the forest keeper

A couple of thugs
bust into a liquor store,
grab some cash,
a few bottles of whisky
and scamper into the forest.

From high up in a tree,
the forest keeper
hears them coming.

As cool as a cucumber,
he shaves stubble from his chin,
takes a sip of coffee,
drops down, scowls:
Fifty dollars to pass!
Pay my toll! *Pay I say*!

One thug points, says:
Get a load of those tights;
and that Mohawk,
what a goof ball;

The forest keeper
hangs his head,
wants nothing more
than to sling
him against the rocks,
but he's bound
by codes of the forest.

So he grabs
a bottle of whisky
from the other thug,
unscrews the lid,
takes a long drink.

the dark room

She enjoys being in the dark room,
watching her brain exit her head and
inflate like a balloon. Her brain coming
from her head doesn't hurt. She wants
to stay in the dark room forever,
watching synapses fire up and sparkle.
Tonight, her brain does something it's
never done before; it turns into a disco
ball over her head, spinning slowly,
throwing light all over the walls and
ceiling. She closes her eyes and allows
things to happen; she drinks the light;
it tastes like sweet cola; she breathes
the light; her lungs crave more. When
there's a knock on the door, her brain
knows the score, deflates and goes
back into her skull. Rubbing her head a
few times to make sure things are
safely tucked away, she takes one more
glance at the dark room, wishing she
could stay for a little while longer.

needing a hand

Sipping cold drinks by the pool,
large wasps swoop down and sting us,
bolting us away to a creepy castle on a
hillside;
inside the castle
the doctor of death
rolls around on a stool,
pushing buttons,
squawking like a hawk,
forecasting,
based on our beating hearts,
how many days we have left.
Is there a trick
to getting out of here?
I understand if you're scared speaking
out,
but search yourself,
clasp hands with the great warriors of
the past,
those who stood with swords extended
on mountains of snow and thunder.
Help us out of here.

nearly

Instead
of working
on the assignment,
the boy focuses,
sticks out his tongue,
draws a picture
of Mickey Mouse.
The teacher
looks over
his shoulder,
says the picture's good
and when
he was his age
he could draw
a mean Daffy Duck.
The boy nearly smiles.
Nearly.

hoping

After a short lecture,
the teacher moves around the room
helping those needing help.

Exhausted, she hopes
there's more to life than this.

She stops at a desk
where her favorite student
fiddles with a nose ring,
chews gum, pops bubbles.

Understand? she says to the girl.
I understand you're a witch, the girl
says,
smirking the way teenagers do.
How dare you, she says,
wanting to yank out the nose ring
and slap her face.

Pretending nothing happened,
she walks toward the window,
wondering
not which laws
she'd broken to get here,
but which laws
she must follow to get out.

a nightmare

Students tie the teacher to a chair, slap
him with floppy notebooks, demand
extra credit on their report cards or
they promise they'll beat him to a
bloody pulp. Since the bloody pulp
style isn't popular, he caves in, allows
the extra credit; who in their right
mind wouldn't? The students let him
loose from the chair and return to their
desks. But it's all a cruel trick, he
knows it, you know it, snow cats in the
mountains of Alaska know it. For a few
minutes they allow him to lecture on
subjects and verbs, but only a few
minutes; paper wads begin pelting and
stinging him in the face. Soon there are
so many paper wads coming he can't
dodge anymore and he gives up trying.
He accepts the pain, figuring he'd done
something in a former life to deserve
it. He goes to his desk, pulls out a
cigarette, and lights up. What's the
worst that can happen?

to my graduating students

All year you've been looking to me for
answers.
Want to know something? I've also been
looking
to you. The way I see it, this learning
gig is a two

way street. If you catch any lesson,
catch this:
answers are found outside the sound of
my voice,
outside words of books, outside the
walls of this

classroom. It's outside in the grime and
slush
you'll find what you're looking for.
Don't worry
about slipping and falling or the scary
moans and

groans you hear; they won't hurt you;
they're
made to intimidate, Before I forget,
I've decided
not to call your parents/ guardians
about the many

afternoons you slept at your desks,
some of you
snoring so loudly I thought your heads

may explode.
We'll keep that between us, a good
memory when

a good memory might be the only thing
left to
get us off the ledge. Good luck
students. Listen
to failure; it has much to say.

counting my lucky stars

Just for fun
I hold up a stereo
crank up the volume
play hip hop music.
The kids love the stuff,
would lick it
like ice cream
if they could.
They look
at me lovingly;
things go well
until a couple
of knuckleheads
throw my chair
through the window.
I yell, but they're fast.
After school
I sit outside
in my chair,
counting my lucky stars
it wasn't me
they'd thrown out there.

failure

I'll just say it:
I was a failure as a middle school
teacher.
Not proud of it.
At times I believe
those kids were creatures
from under the sea,
and other times,
creatures sent here from Pluto.
Regardless where they were from,
or what their cruel intentions were
(and they were cruel)
I was a failure as a middle school
teacher
and there's nothing anyone can do
about it.

memory

After being criticized in class for one thing or another, the kid plans on killing the teacher after school with a pencil. He's got it all planned, an escape route, a place to lay low for a year or two. The only thing holding him back is a memory he has from a few months ago at his mother's funeral. Arriving with a bouquet of roses, the teacher put an arm around his shoulder, said he was sorry and if he ever needed anything let him know. The memory saved many lives that day.

a tiny spider

a tiny spider
climbs a web
strung between
branches of a tree,
climbs until
lost among leaves;
a tiny spider
gone to a secret place
designed for
secrecy.

his little tree

Please don't
cut down his little tree.
It may be nearly dead,
but it's a safe place.
He hears birds as they land
on the dry branches,
and they hear him,
every song, every sigh.
They share the wind
of each other's
flights and falls.
He needs a win.
Please don't
cut down his little tree.

a drop of dew

a drop
of dew
on a blade
of grass;
sunlight
giving it color,
a breeze, life.

twigs

A bunch
of birds
bounce across
twigs in a tree.
The poor things
deserve more,
not the silly birds,
but the twigs.

a quick break

Desperately
needing a break
from the crowd,
she leaves her coffee cup,
walks outside,
finds a calm place
to sit under a tree.
As if trying
to touch stars,
she reaches up;
rain drips
from leaves
onto her body.
she feels clean,
ready to face anything.

like us

It's no
crime listening
to the stars;
they mean no harm.
Like us
they must
get awfully lonely.
they've done
so much
for us already,
the least we can do
is let them
get whatever
it is off their minds;
we owe them that.

encouragement

He usually enjoys
spending time writing,
feeling a good paragraph or two
worthy of tropical drinks;
But he's not naïve;
he understands
his writing is usually trash,
perfect for feeding fires
on frosty nights.
No big deal; nothing's perfect.
The act of sucking junk
from his dirty system,
slinging it onto paper,
making sense from it,
helps him make sense of his life.
When he totally messes up,
hates his life
and what he writes,
don't leave him hanging,
give the poor guy a hug
or a fist bump;
you'll be glad
when the time comes
for you to go through the same.

writing style

I write from the gut,
let it rest, go back and revise.
Usually the revised writing is better,
but sometimes, oddly enough,
the original draft is best.
Wish there was a recipe,
you know, simple instructions
for a perfect piece of writing;
trust me, I've looked
and haven't stumbled on anything yet;
Maybe it doesn't exist.
For now I'll stick
to the theory that the secret
of good writing is hard work;
sounds nice anyway.
All I have left to do
is what I've been doing for some time:
flip another coin,
decide what's complete
and what needs more work.

prayers

This morning I pray
in the Tennessee hills;

the prayer chooses to
stay in the hills instead

of flying straight away.
I don't blame it

for wanting to catch a
break and stay in the

the hills for a while,
as long as it goes

where it needs to go
so my struggles can be

heard and a plan of action
sorted. Knowing me and

spiritual things like prayer
are similar is comforting,

makes me feel like I have
a great shot at this after-
life thing.

it's all good

She's a writer,
standing on a crate
under the full moon,
waving her wand
like a conductor,
without any idea how she got there
or if she'll return;
she slings charms and spells
through the night;
some catch; some don't.
throwing back her head
she roars without shame;
disturbed,
the moon quakes,
cracks into pieces.
Getting the pain
out had to be done
or she would've cracked too;
it's not bad; it's all good.
A comet shoots
through the sky
as she stands on the crate
waving the wand,
holding out her tongue
for the milky flakes
of moon falling like feathers.
She's a writer
and no longer cares who knows it.

no good

If you're bored silly
trying to read this,
perhaps thinking about ripping
an ear off and mailing it to a
mother-in-law,
don't freak out.
Hang in there;
Give it a fair shake.
Granted,
I'm not the best writer in the world,
just the way it is.
I need something,
strong coffee,
a slice of lemon pie,
an ear-piercing guitar solo
from Pink Floyd.
My friend,
the real reason I've written you is:
do you have any music
or movies you could slide my way?
My pantry's bare.
It would mean the world right about
now.
If you don't I completely understand;
For all you know,
I'm a raving lunatic
waiting to gobble you up
once you enter my living room.
And that's no good,
no good at all.

a problem with the internet

As much as I've tried,
as late as I've stayed up,
I'm still unable
to buy a trip
to Heaven
through the Internet.
Eggs I can get,
bacon,
shirts and shoes,
even a house,
but not a trip of Heaven.
What's the big secret?
The deep conspiracy?
My hope
is the next time
I'm surfing the Internet,
a light will pop
on my computer,
displaying a quote
for a one-way trip to heaven.
Relax, I'm not getting
my hopes up too high.

like a song

She's young and confused and needs
help;
She can't hide her feelings any longer;

Trembling, she steps out of the closet
holding a knife. She prays she won't be

punished too hard for things out of her
control. But something like a song
knocks

the knife from her hand. A few years
later,
she gives birth. Holding her baby boy
close,

she hears a song. She whispers, *thank
you.*

for you

when things
get super scary
(which they will)
don't freak out;
look up;
that's me
out there
in the mist,
calling like crazy,
hair spiked,
wearing the same
leather jacket
I've worn forever,
still pretending
to be cool
for you.

stanza

The young poet goes into his room and lights a candle and finishes writing a poem: *in the valley/ the mist above/ I slowly dissolve/ never to be with my friends*. He plunges a dagger into his stomach, falls to the floor. He awakens in a raft on a rough sea. Looking up, he sees another version of the stanza he'd written in his room before killing himself: *at the summit/the mist below/I quickly dissolve/to be with my friends*. Aware this is different from what he'd written before taking his life, all he can do is hold tightly to the side of the raft. The next time he reads the stanza, however, he totally falls in love with it, even sings it aloud. Finding the mountain in the distance, he jumps out of the raft and swims for it. Safely making it, he climbs to the summit, dissolves like fog to be with his friends. But the stanza remains, a beacon for others, a blazing promise that great things are near.

break through

Find your wings,
your flap,
and take off;
turn back
and you're lost.
Keep going,
break through;
salvation
with a warm hug
and a tender kiss
is there.

dying

I'm dying
to fling
off this body,
allow my true self
to stretch
and start its slide
across the bright dance
floor in the sky,
onward past
everything imagined.

www.ingramcontent.com/pod-product-compliance
Lightning Source LLC
Chambersburg PA
CBHW071907020426
42331CB00010B/2708